SILENCE IS NOT AN OPTION

YOU CAN IMPACT THE WORLD FOR CHANGE

STUART LAWRENCE

SCHOLASTIC

To my son, Theo, who is ten today, as I write this. I will never be that cool superhero I would love you to see me as but I know in time that you will grow into a great and wonderful man and your light will shine bright for ever, as you remind me so much of Stephen.

SL 2021

Published in the UK by Scholastic Children's Books, 2021
Euston House, 24 Eversholt Street, London, NW1 1DB
Scholastic Ltd Ireland offices at: Unit 89E, Lagan Road, Dublin Industrial Estate,
Glasnevin, Dublin 11.

A division of Scholastic Limited
London ~ New York ~ Toronto ~ Sydney ~ Auckland
Mexico City ~ New Delhi ~ Hong Kong

Text © Stuart Lawrence, 2021
Author photograph © Simon Fredericks

The right of Stuart Lawrence to be identified as the author and illustrator of this work
has been asserted by him under the Copyright, Designs and Patents Act 1988.

ISBN 978 07023 1056 0

A CIP catalogue record for this book is
available from the British Library.

Printed in the UK by Bell and Bain Ltd, Glasgow

Any website addresses listed in the book are correct at the time of going to print.
However, please be aware that online content is subject to change and websites can contain
or offer content that is unsuitable for children. We advise all children be supervised when
using the internet.

Papers used by Scholastic Children's Books are made from wood grown in
sustainable forests.

2 4 6 8 10 9 7 5 3 1

www.scholastic.co.uk

CONTENTS

INTRODUCTION

W e all want to be successful in life and to be remembered for our achievements – but how can we do that, when the world can seem so big and sometimes scary?

In this book I want to give you the tools to live a successful, positive and happy life. I want to encourage you to create change in the world, no matter how small or big.

Role Models

T he people we find inspirational change as we grow up. When I was a kid, my role model was John Barnes, who played football for Liverpool. At the time, Liverpool was top of the league. Like most of the kids my age, I decided that they were the team I wanted to support (I'm now an Arsenal fan and have been since I was 14!). I really looked up to John Barnes for a few reasons. Firstly, he looked like me. Secondly, he loved football like me and, most importantly, he was good at it. I felt I had found someone I could hope to be like when I grew up. I admired his characteristics and wanted to take on some of them for myself. Almost everybody liked him, and most of us want to be well liked.

my

RO

When I was a kid, my role model was John Barnes

LE
model

In 1993, when I was a teenager, a major event happened in my life. My big brother, Stephen Lawrence, was tragically murdered in a racially motivated attack. For a few readers, this might be the first time you've heard of Stephen. Some of you might have a big brother or sister and know how amazing it is to have one. It's great having someone to look up to, do things with and grow up with. As younger siblings, we often try to copy our big brothers and sisters and try to be as good as them. This was how I was with my brother, Stephen. I admired him like you would admire a superhero. For Stephen to become the victim of a racist murder was a massive blow for me. It was something I never imagined could happen. There were six attackers and it wasn't until 2012 that two of the attackers were jailed.

When I was told what had happened, I went through a rush of emotions: sadness, anger, shock, disbelief and confusion. I wanted to try and find out what had happened. I felt I could help in some way and would walk down the road where the murder took place, playing everything over in my mind. Looking back, that probably wasn't the best way of coping, but it was the way I dealt with losing my brother at the time.

This experience isn't something I tell people when I first meet them because I think if you like me as Stuart then that's cool. I want people to get to know me because of the person I am.

Meeting Nelson Mandela

Not long after Stephen's death, my family and I had the privilege of meeting Nelson Mandela. For those of you who don't know Nelson Mandela, he led a movement that fought for the rights of black people in South Africa and between 1990 and 1994 led negotiations that ended the separation of black and white people, also known as 'apartheid'. Nelson Mandela spent most of his life fighting for people's rights, even when he was imprisoned for 27 years. He had only been a free man for three years when we met him and it made me think, wow, he didn't need to meet us because I'm sure there were so many other things he wanted to do with his newfound freedom. Yet here he was, selflessly helping our community. His presence really changed my brother's case. He became an inspiration to me, and I felt even more inspired after I read his autobiography. For Nelson Mandela, silence was never an option.

We need more strong adult role models like Nelson leading the way.

Silence is Not an Option

Silence is not and should not be an option, especially when we know right from wrong. Before Nelson Mandela came along, the media were making out that Stephen was a drug-dealing gang member. When Nelson Mandela spoke out, the world learned who he really was – an A-level student, trying to achieve his dream of becoming an architect.

We need more strong adult role models like Nelson leading the way.

WHO ARE YOU DOING IT FOR?

Do you want to be successful for yourself? For your family? Or do you want to be successful so that people around you think you are successful?

We are living in the age of social media, where everyone sees everything. Our natural instinct is to show our followers everything we're doing, but you should ask yourself why you're doing it. Is it for you, or is it for someone else?

When I think of success and achieving my goals, I sometimes ask myself, "Who am I doing it for?" The first person I think of is my son. Before he was born, I looked at the world very differently. After his birth, everything changed. I started thinking less about myself and more about how I could help him to become a superstar. I want him to be happy with whatever it is he decides to do in life. I am constantly trying to be a better person so I can be the best role model I can be for my son – to create and inspire change. The reason I keep going and keep reaching is to light that fire of self-confidence and self-worth in my son. I want to show him that all goals he sets are worth chasing, building towards and achieving.

I want to help you think about your future and lead you to make great choices. But what are the keys to success? Each chapter in this book will cover one of these – a tool for you to understand and use in a positive way, to help your voice be heard and to help you stand out from the crowd.

THESE TOOLS ARE:

CHAPTER 1: YOU ARE YOUR OWN SUPERHERO

Building self-confidence – if you don't champion yourself, who will?

CHAPTER 2: PERSONALITY, PASSION, PURPOSE

Getting to know yourself – discover what pushes you and how to use this to your advantage.

CHAPTER 3: YOU ARE IN CONTROL

Improving self-control – understanding self-control so you can steer yourself to success.

CHAPTER 4: WHAT ATTITUDE?

Choosing a positive attitude – realizing attitude is everything and with the right one you can make it to the top.

CHAPTER 5: IT'S NOT FAILURE, IT'S UNFINISHED BUSINESS

Learning from failure – discover that failure is actually achieving, because we learn from it.

CHAPTER 6: DREAM BIG

Setting yourself goals – firing up your imagination so you can reach for the stars.

CHAPTER 7: TAKE YOUR TIME

Managing your time – using your time wisely so you're not late for success.

CHAPTER 8: WHAT IS WEALTH?

Making money – money isn't everything but it's important to understand money and the world of work.

CHAPTER 9: LIFELONG LEARNING

Choosing to learn – learning doesn't just happen in the classroom, it's happening all around you.

Once you reach the end of this book, I want you to have the tools and guidance to become successful and to lead a life full of positivity.

→posi

tivity

CHAPTER

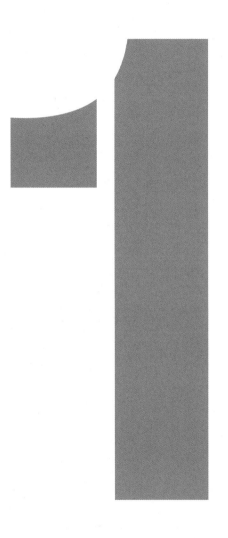

YOU ARE YOUR OWN SUPERHERO

ALL OF US ARE UNIQUE

After Stephen's murder, I asked myself what my big brother would want me to do. How would he want me to act? I knew he would want me to follow my ambitions and be the greatest I could be, so I put my cape on and charged on in his memory. With my superhero cape on, I set myself goals and achieved them one by one.

My superpowers
(the things I'm really good at):

★ Cooking

★ Helping other people

★ Art

★ Complimenting others

Now, I want to talk about you. What are you all about? What would you say your superpowers are? Where do you want to go in life? Don't worry if you're not quite sure yet.

The Biggest Competitor You Will Have in Life is YOU

All of us are unique. We have different personalities, strengths, weaknesses and habits. But these differences are something to celebrate and use to our advantage. Try not to compare yourself to other people too much. It's impossible to be the same as anyone else, so it's pointless trying. The world would be a boring place if we were all the same!

Grab a notepad and answer the following questions:

1. What are you good at?
2. What matters most to you?
3. What do you want to achieve in the next ten years?
4. What do you have a passion for?
5. Does it matter what others think about you?
6. When did you last push the boundaries and get out of your comfort zone?

After doing this activity, you should be able to see right in front of you what is important to you. You'll be starting to get a sense of where you want to go in life. Hopefully, you're beginning to understand what you could achieve if you push yourself.

You are still developing and growing, so try not to make decisions now that might make you miss out on opportunities in the future. For example, if you want to be an actor, you might say to yourself, "It doesn't really matter if I put 100 per cent effort into my maths exams, so long as I try hard in drama." However, you could find that, when you start out in your acting career, it's tough to get regular jobs straight away. Not having those maths skills might make it harder for you to find a part-time job to tide you over until you can build up regular acting work. You might even discover you don't like acting as much as you thought you did, and it turns out accountancy is your calling.

Never-ending Goal Setting

It is good to set goals. Setting goals helps you to focus on what it is you really want and understand why you might have to make sacrifices to achieve it. For example, you might want to become the fastest runner at running club and win the next race. To become that runner, you will have to make sacrifices. You'll need to put in lots of practice, drink more water and eat healthily.

It is good to set GOALS

Setting GOALS helps you to focus

Sometimes, you'll have to choose to do these things even when you don't feel like it.

But what happens after you have reached your goal? Could you go another round? Could you beat another level? If we didn't keep going, level by level, we would all be living in caves, sheltering from the rain and no longer advancing. So, once you've won a race, what next? You might then set a goal of becoming the fastest local runner. Then what? You might start training to enter a national competition, then maybe even the Olympics. The goals go on and on and on.

Humble Self-confidence

It's important to have self-confidence – to trust in your own skills, qualities and judgements. However, it's important to be humble at the same time. There's a thin line between being self-confident and coming across as full of yourself.

Having self-confidence as a young person helps you to make safe and sensible decisions. It also helps you to avoid people or situations that might be harmful to you. Throughout life, different things can affect your self-confidence. It could be **positively** affected by passing your exams or **negatively** affected if you fall out with a friend. Below are a few easy ways to boost your self-confidence:

★ Fake it until you make it

Imagine the person you want to become and portray that person to those around you. To go back to the example of becoming a runner, you might be nervous before your big race. But if you march on to that field and start stretching at the start line like a true athlete, chances are you'll have everyone convinced, which will make you feel more confident in turn.

★ Think positive

Try and train your mind to think positively. It can be small things to start off with like, doing your hair and saying to yourself, "Hey, I look really nice this morning!" or taking the time to notice some pretty flowers. Eventually, this positive attitude about the small things will carry over to bigger things in your life.

★ Act positive

Not only do you have to practise thinking positively, but you also need to put those thoughts and feelings into action. Choose not to be silent and speak up for yourself – and speak up for others, too. If you see a friend is feeling down, try to cheer them up. If a friend has done something good, praise them, lift them up and empower them.

SPEAK UP FOR YOURSELF – AND SPEAK UP FOR OTHERS, TOO

★ Dress well to feel good

When we dress nicely or wear our favourite clothes we generally tend to feel better about ourselves. Trying a different hairstyle can be fun, too. It's about having the power to make yourself feel comfortable and good. The more control you can take of your life, the better it can make you feel.

★ Stand tall

When we stand tall, we have the feeling of being in charge. To put this into practice, imagine there is a piece of string connected to your head, pulling it up to the sky and straightening out the rest of your body.

★ Smile more

Smile and the world smiles with you. Try this out the next time you are in a new situation: just relax and smile at someone and it's quite likely they'll smile back.

★ Exercise

Exercise will pop up a few times in this book but that should only show you how important it is. Getting your heart racing and your muscles moving is a great way to boost your mood. When you exercise it releases endorphins, dopamine and adrenaline, which are all brain chemicals connected to feelings of happiness and confidence. Exercise also makes you feel less stressed. It's a win-win activity!

The Superhero of Your Family

The things that your family say and do have an effect on you. These effects can be both positive and negative but everything you experience is a lesson. Some of you may have a family that expects only the highest of achievements from you and you feel incredibly pressured. Some of you may have a family that is not so pressured and you sort of feel there isn't any expectation at all.

Having and building up self-confidence can help you in so many different ways. Most importantly, when you have a good sense of self-confidence you can feel powerful – like you can do and achieve anything. You can be the superhero of your family.

There are some things we are asked to do, that we dislike. We might feel there is no need for it or we just point blank don't want to do it. I personally hate sweeping up leaves because it's almost an endless task but my dad always made me do this chore when I was younger. Was there a lesson my dad was trying to teach me there? Thinking back, I feel like he was trying to teach me values – that you need to be a neat and tidy person not only in the home but also outside the home, and that the way you carry yourself and present yourself can take you a long way in life.

In the past, whatever your father did for a job, you might also do as an adult. However, times have changed and

29

it is okay now for you to have different passions to your family. As long as you are respectful about where you are coming from then it will get you to where you are going. This is not to say your past and family history is what defines you, but it is important to understand where you come from and be respectful of it. For example, your father might own a construction business where it is has always been a tradition for all sons to work in the business too. BUT you do not have an interest in construction or a passion for it. This is okay. As long as you approach the situation respectfully, speak to your parents about what your passions are and what you would like to do in life, there is no reason why you shouldn't follow your dreams.

Privilege

Now, looking at the superhero you are or can be, there is another little superpower called privilege. Do you know what privilege is? Some of us are born with it and some of us have to work hard to achieve it. Privilege is having an advantage that other people may not have, for example, person A could be born into a family who doesn't have a lot of money and lives in a poor area of the country, and person B could be born into a rich family, living in an area full of mansions. Person B was clearly born into privilege, BUT that does not mean that Person A cannot work hard to move into a position of privilege themselves.

Let's take a look at Zaha Hadid. She was born in 1950

to an upper-class family in Iraq, which allowed her to study during a time when not many women were able to do so in her home country. By using her position of privilege and by working hard, Zaha become one of the most famous and influential architects of the twentieth and twenty-first centuries. She was the first woman to win the very special 'Pritzder Architecture Prize', along with lots of other awards.

Coming from a wealthy family didn't automatically mean Zaha would have it easy, as the world of architecture was then dominated by men. However, she inspired young girls and women to follow their dreams of becoming an architect by showing them that you can achieve goals and break down barriers if you persevere.

How boring the world would be if we didn't have some of Zaha's amazing buildings planted around the world!

There is an old saying that goes, "The same boiling water that softens the potato, hardens the egg." It means that life is not always about our circumstances, but what we make of those circumstances. People can be quick to come up with excuses about why they have not achieved something, but there will be others who are in the same situation as them, or an even worse one, who still work hard to achieve their goals. Remember there is always something small that we can be thankful for.

Being Polite, Being Kind

Don't you just hate it when you hold the door open for someone and they don't say thank you? As the saying goes, manners cost nothing. In my opinion, manners have helped me more in life than anything else. Good manners make people feel more comfortable around you. You could even say being polite is a superpower!

Beyond being polite, one of the greatest superpowers a person can have is being kind. Even small things, like sharing a smile with someone, offering to help someone with their bags or giving a compliment to someone can go a really long way. These kindnesses can even help to boost other people's self-confidence. What small act of kindness were you once shown that you will never forget? Did it boost your self-confidence?

When people do kind things for us, it's important to say. thank you. I was about 22 when I first realized the number of sacrifices my mum had made to help me get to where I wanted to be in life. I picked up the phone and called her to let her know how much I appreciated her and to say thank you. Perhaps now would be a good time for you to find someone who has made sacrifices for you, to let them know you appreciate their help and support. Let's celebrate all the superheroes in our life, who help us become superheroes, too.

You are only ever in competition with yourself. There may

be someone else doing, or wanting to do, some of the same things in life, but their purpose or approach may be different. You have something to offer that nobody else can. Be confident in your superpowers and use them to do good things in the world.

Focus on yourself and you will be successful.

CHAPTER

PERSONALITY, PASSION, PURPOSE

IT'S ALL ABOUT EXPLORING THE GOOD BITS OF YOUR CHARACTER

Stephen was someone everyone wanted to be like. He was good at everything he put his mind to. He was also super popular and really creative. Sometimes, when we were with my friends, it was as if he was more popular with them than I was! However, he always looked after me and made sure I was okay. He was a typical big brother.

This chapter is about understanding and knowing yourself so that you can make the most of your personality, passion and purpose. It's all about exploring the good bits of your character and then finding out how to use them to become successful in life. Your characteristics – those building blocks that make you, you – affect everything you do, so it's really important to get to know them.

Personality and Characteristics

So where does your personality come from? Well some of your character is handed down from your parents. In the same way our skin colour or hair texture is influenced by our genes, so is our behaviour. But that doesn't mean we are born with a ready-made personality. As we grow up, our character changes because of what we experience and the people we meet. We pick up different quirks and personality traits from family and friends, and are shaped by the world around us. As our personality is always changing and developing, that also means we can work on parts of our personality that might be holding us back.

Now, let's say you are a person who doesn't feel very confident. Do you think that is a characteristic you can learn to change?

Yes, it is!

Using a notepad, I want you to write down some characteristics you think you have. **Here are mine:**

1. Ambitious
2. Competitive
3. Determined
4. Friendly
5. Generous
6. Hopeful
7. Imaginative
8. Easily distracted
9. Loyal
10. Inquisitive
11. Respectful
12. Self-confident
13. Shy
14. Trustworthy
15. Open

This activity should help you focus in on the great bits about your personality. It should also help you to think about any negative characteristics you might have. As I said previously, characteristics are things you can learn to change. Do you have any negative traits that you'd like to change?

Everyone is Unique – Everyone is Valuable

Sometimes, we meet people who are similar to us. They may like the same music as us, watch the same TV series as us or enjoy the same books as us, so it's easy to become friends. But sometimes, we meet people who are not so like us. They might like different sports or different music, or live in a different kind of home, but that doesn't mean we can't become friends anyway. You might learn something from one another or have positive personality traits that rub off on each other.

Don't be afraid to surround yourself with all kinds of different people. If you struggle with a subject at school, why not spend some time with the kids who love it? Try to find out why they are so passionate about something you find tricky. Let's say you're struggling with maths and just can't get your head around division or times tables, but there's a kid in your class who just gets it, without even trying. Why not reach out and take the first steps to becoming friends with them? By spending time with them, you might begin to understand why they love maths so much, and you might even begin to enjoy it. They might push you to discover a hidden talent. Perhaps you'll push them to discover one, too.

It's important to celebrate and embrace differences. Being open to speaking with and hanging out with people who might not look like you, speak like you or have the same characteristics as you is so important. Our personalities are always growing and changing.

DON'T BE AFRAID TO SURROUND YOURSELF WITH ALL KINDS OF DIFFERENT PEOPLE

Pick Your Passion

Your passion is usually the thing that pushes you to succeed at something. If you try to do something you don't really have a passion for, you won't put the same amount of effort in compared to something you do have a passion for. For example, I like to ice skate, but I don't have the determination to push through the bruises and possible broken bones. I don't think, therefore, I can be the next Surya Bonaly or Richard Ewell; I don't have the passion for it.

Passion can push you through hard times. If you have a passion for something, you'll do whatever it takes to become better. You might not be sure what your passion is just yet. Don't worry if that's the case! Did you know we often find our passions through different experiences, as we get older? For example, you might quite like science at primary school, but it's only when you get to secondary school that you discover it's biology, specifically, that you're really keen on. Or perhaps you enjoy going on theatre trips with your class. After one show, maybe you get to go backstage, meet the actors and see how it all works. Perhaps through those experiences you discover you have a passion for acting and drama.

It takes a while to get really good at something, even if you're passionate about it. You are not going to be the best footballer, mathematician, coder or swimmer straight away. But that doesn't mean you won't be fantastic at your passion one day.

Setbacks and failures are helpful

– through them we learn what we need to do to succeed. This is where your mindset becomes super important!

grow
min

th
dset

Meet Your Mindset

Your 'mindset' means your way of thinking. It's better for your future if you can be open to new challenges and ideas with a **'growth mindset'** than closed off with a **'fixed mindset'**. When you have a fixed mindset, you believe you can't change. With a fixed mindset, you might not be letting your character, intelligence and talents grow or develop.

Here are some examples of things someone with a **fixed mindset** might think:

Feedback is bad – it makes me feel like I'm not good enough.

I don't like to be challenged.

I stick to what I know.

I give up easily.

I can either do it or I can't.

I am either good at it or I'm not.

Imagine you are learning to ride a bike. You might try to get started and fall off. If you have a fixed mindset, you might give up, feeling like you will never be able to succeed. You won't try and push yourself to get through the challenges you are facing. You decide bike riding just isn't for you. You can't do it.

If you have a growth mindset, however, you see challenges as opportunities to grow and become better. You'll understand that you can improve your talents and abilities by pushing yourself. In other words, you'll get back on the bike.

Here are some examples of things someone with a **growth mindset** might think:

I love feedback – how would I improve without it?

I like to be challenged.

I like trying new things.

I don't give up easily.

I can learn to do anything I want.

I don't mind making mistakes. That's often how I get good at something.

Here's another example of why having a growth mindset is great. In football, playing one-on-one is an essential part of the game. It is something coaches like their players to practise a lot. Being able to use a skill or trick to evade other players, stop them from getting the ball and then score a goal is the whole point of the game. When you first start learning to play football, you might be able to complete a skill or trick when you are by yourself. As soon as you get into a real game, however, it all goes to pieces! Maybe it's the extra pressure, the change in the environment, the shouting crowd... Whatever the reason, you just can't seem to get the ball past any players.

With a fixed mindset, your solution might be to give up and try another sport. But a growth mindset pushes you to keep trying. Even if you try and fail ten times over. With a growth mindset, you might realize that it would be more useful to practise against a real person, rather than on your own. The process you go through by failing is what will make you a brilliant footballer in the future. This is how players become the best in their field. With a growth mindset, you will tell yourself that you need to keep going. The harder it is to get past your opponent, the more you will improve.

> # Every time you fail, you will be able to learn something from it.

Get That Growth Mindset Growing

There are so many good things about having a growth mindset. You start to focus on what you could do to improve, instead of worrying about what you might have done wrong. You will aim to work hard and learn more, because when you have a growth mindset you love challenges.

Do you think you have a fixed mindset or a growth mindset at the moment? Even if you have more of a fixed mindset right now, don't worry. Here are a few ways you could get that mindset growing:

★ Look at challenges as opportunities

Attack a small challenge until you learn how to succeed. Think about it like a game on your tablet or console; to get to level three you have to get through level one and two first. Do you give up on the whole game if you fail a level? No, you keep trying because you want to get to the next stage of the game. If you give up on challenges in life too soon, you might never see the 'next stage' – at the end of the day, it's you who misses out. For example, if you give up the first time you fall off your bike, you will never be able to master a wheelie.

★ Work on your weaknesses

If we hide from our weaknesses then we will never beat them. Pick a weakness and work to make it better. You might not be good at your times tables, which might make you dislike maths. But if you stick at them until you get better, you can move on to a different area of maths that you might enjoy more. Once you improve one weakness, you will get a sense of achievement that will hopefully inspire you to work on another of your weaknesses.

★ Swap the word 'failing' with 'learning'

When you make a mistake or you don't achieve a goal, this isn't a failure. You have just learned something new. You've just learned what doesn't work. If you think about why and how things went wrong, that will help you to get it right next time. Again, like a game on your tablet or console, you'll only find out the right moves to get you to the next level from trying the wrong ones.

★ Embrace growth before speed

Learning fast isn't the same as learning well. We are always in competition to do everything first – to be the quickest or the best. Sometimes, however, we need to give ourselves time. We need to slow down and put in the effort to study something properly, even if that means spending an hour less with our friends, and an hour longer with a book.

★ Bad feedback is good feedback

I don't want to make you roll your eyes, but not all critical feedback is bad. The next time someone gives you feedback, instead of becoming frustrated or defensive, sit down and think about what the person has said. See if you can pick out points that will help you to improve, so you can get more positive feedback next time.

The Power of Purpose

A purpose is a reason, or the 'why', behind what we do. Passions can change on a whim, but your purpose is much more focused. Passions come and go, whereas your purpose tends to be long term. A purpose can appear in lots of different forms; perhaps you want to save our planet's wildlife by slowing down climate change, or to travel the world to help children in need, or to become a lawyer to help fight for human rights. For some people, finding a sense of purpose can be confusing and difficult. For others, it will come more naturally.

What's your purpose? Or what do you think it could be?

A good way of finding your purpose in life is to speak to new people. Though it might be scary to speak to other people outside of your friendship group, it can open your eyes to activities, hobbies, experiences and even jobs you might never have thought about. Explore your interests, think about the things you like to talk about and pursue the activities you enjoy; these things might give you that feeling of purpose.

Using your notepad, try and answer these questions:

- What are your hobbies?
- What do you like to talk about with your family and friends?
- What activities make you feel happy when you are doing them?

By doing this activity, you'll get thinking about what you are interested in, what you like and what you really, really like! Then, hopefully, you can focus in on these things to find your feeling of purpose.

Once you discover your purpose, it will give you a direction in life.

A PURPOSE IS A REASON

Your Moral Compass

In life we face lots of hard decisions. Should you copy your friend's homework? Should you be nice to your little sister, even though she's annoying you? Should you take the last snack and blame it on your dog? In situations like this, your moral compass helps you to judge what is right and wrong. Like a real-life compass that helps you to find your way, your moral compass guides you to make the correct decision.

Having a strong moral compass is really important.

Your moral compass helps you to make good decisions. You can make sure it is up to scratch by chatting to someone else – this is what I like to call **'the buddy system'**. When you need some guidance, or someone to chat through a problem with, you could talk to your best friend, cousin, uncle, auntie or anyone else you trust. Together, you can figure out what the right thing to do is.

The people around us can improve our moral compass. For example, a friend might pull you to the side and call you out on something you are doing that is wrong, like cheating in class or being nasty to another student. This might be uncomfortable at the time, but most likely your friend has your best interests at heart.

The people around us can also negatively influence our moral compass. A friend might encourage you to lie to your parents about missing the bus so you can stay out past your curfew. Morally, you know it's wrong for you to do this and that it's disrespectful to your parents. However, it's really easy to let our moral compass slip if we don't have people around us who are being positive influences. You have to be firm in knowing what is right and wrong. Try to surround yourself with like-minded people, who will positively support and influence your decisions.

Here's something for you to think about. Imagine there is someone in your class at school that is not treated very nicely by others in your year group. One breaktime, you hear some people calling them nasty names. Knowing what is right and wrong, would you stick up for that person?

Would you report the bullying to a teacher? Or would you be silent and continue with your day as if you didn't see anything? Choosing not to be silent and speaking up for someone can massively affect that person's life. By making the choice not to be silent, you can help their self-confidence and make school a happier place for them.

We Are Always Growing

My first passion was acting. This passion came from watching my aunties who were part of a dance group. We would go to their yearly shows and it inspired me to try to have my own career in the arts. As I grew up, my passions changed. Even though I didn't end up becoming an actor, I did work in the world of art, in graphic design. I taught graphic design for fifteen years, before I found a new passion. Now I work to create change for young people. As you can see, our passions are always changing and growing with us and this is okay!

Now you've discovered a bit more about your personality, passion and purpose, you've gained some powerful tools that can be used for positive action and change. Look back at the questions you answered on page 52 and think about ways you could feed your personality, passion and purpose, perhaps through taking part in activities related to your hobbies. Let your passions shine through and do not silence yourself – celebrate those things that make you, you.

REMEMBER,

SILENCE
IS NOT AN
OPTION

CHAPTER

YOU
ARE IN
CONTROL

SELF-CONTROL

After losing my brother Stephen, I really had to learn self-control. Suddenly, my family and I were in the newspapers and on the TV. A lot of the time, the public were being misinformed about our story. I was so angry that my brother was being portrayed as a gang member and a drug dealer, when he was an A-level student aspiring to become an architect.

However, I had to control myself, because lashing out would only affect my family and my brother's case negatively. It didn't mean I didn't speak out, but I had to exercise self-control in the way I handled the situation. I had to be calm and composed, even though I didn't feel like it.

What is Self-control?

Having self-control means being able to manage your decisions, emotions and behaviours so that you can achieve your goals. This skill is what separates humans from the rest of the animal kingdom!

Self-control is rooted in the front part of our brains, in an area called the prefrontal cortex. This is the planning, problem-solving and decision-making centre of the brain. Did you know that this part of the brain is much larger in humans than it is in other mammals? This area of our brain acts differently at different stages of our lives. For example, teenagers are more likely to act on impulse or to misunderstand their emotions than older people. As much as you might not want to believe us adults and feel like you are an exception to the rule, these are scientific facts!

You can only control yourself. For example, let's say you are trying out to become the captain of the school netball team and, unfortunately, you aren't picked for the role. Instead of sulking, getting angry or upset, you show good sportsmanship and shake the hand of your competitor. In doing this, you use your self-control. You are unable to control the situation but you are able to control your reaction and that is what is important. Don't forget, it's always useful to get feedback so that you can improve and win next time.

MANAGE YOUR DECISIONS, EMOTIONS AND BEHAVIOURS SO THAT YOU CAN ACHIEVE YOUR GOALS

Self-control Skills

We all think we are the only ones who have a little voice inside our heads. You know, the one that sometimes says unhelpful things like: **"I'm not the best at that so there's no point in doing it"** or **"I can't run that fast, so I'm not going to enter the race."** But I want you to know that EVERYONE has that voice, and it can be helpful, too. It can be the voice that tells us not to give up on our homework, even if we're tired, or to push that little bit harder in a football match. We can listen to that voice and make a judgement about whether it's encouraging us or holding us back. Remember, you are always in control of yourself.

Using your notepad, I want you to jot down a few things:

1. Give two examples of when you didn't practise self-control and what the negative results were. For example, maybe you didn't stop chatting in class one day and got detention.

2. Now imagine you have a chance to go back and change things. Write down how you could have handled the situation better. What would the results have been if you had used self-control?

Thinking again about this example, you could write: *after the teacher asked me to stop talking, I did as I was asked. I didn't have to waste my time sitting in detention, so I went to the park to play football with my friends instead.*

Screen Time

It's easy to get stuck in front of a screen. Even I find myself binge-watching a Netflix series or using my phone for long periods of time. I have to practise self-control and get back to the real world. Wasting your time staring at a screen for too long can distract you from things that could make you the best version of yourself. It can be helpful to set some rules. My family and I timetable how much screen time we have, so that we can make sure it doesn't take over our lives and distract us from our goals.

We all use our phones, tablets and computers for absolutely everything, from contacting each other to searching for homework help, playing games to keeping up to date with the news. Quite often, this constant access to screens can scramble our thoughts without us even realizing. With our whole lives built around technology, it can be incredibly hard to tear ourselves away from the screen. Once you practise self-control and fill your time with other activities, such as doing exercise, enjoying a hobby or talking to your family, it will become much easier.

Here are some great reasons why you should definitely not jump on your phone as soon as you wake up:

- It increases symptoms of stress, anxiety and depression.
- It wastes time and stops you from getting on with something useful.
- You get your brain ready for distraction for the rest of the day.
- Using social media apps can cause you to compare yourself to other people.

Ways you can break the routine of using your phone during the first hour of waking up:

- exercising
- making a healthy breakfast
- journalling/writing in a diary
- setting goals for your day, even if they are small.

I want to challenge you to try not to use a screen for the first hour of your day for one week. Each day, write down what you have done during that hour instead of staring at a screen. If you have a phone, you could try putting it on flight mode before you go to bed. That way, you won't wake up to loads of messages or social media notifications.

Using your phone or a screen in the hour before going to bed also has a negative impact:

- Using a screen before bed keeps your mind awake, so it'll take you longer to get to sleep. Less sleep means you could feel short-tempered and less energetic the next day.

- Your phone gives off a special kind of light, called blue light. Blue light overpowers your melatonin, the hormone in your body that controls your sleep. When your body is low on melatonin, it struggles to get to sleep. Too much blue light can also damage your eyes.

- The buzzes and pings of your phone can mess with your mind, even when you're asleep. They can interrupt your sleep cycles, meaning you get less deep sleep. This can affect your creativity and problem-solving skills.

Here are some things you could do instead of using a screen in the hour before going to bed:

★ Gentle exercise

Do some stretching on your bedroom floor, or go for a jog around the garden if you have one. Be gentle with yourself though, remember this is the time to unwind and get ready to relax and go to sleep.

★ Reading

Studies show that reading for at least six minutes before you go to bed lowers stress by 68 per cent! It gets the body ready for sleep and relaxes the muscles. Plus, it boosts brainpower and creativity.

★ Journalling/writing in a diary

Spending a bit of time jotting down some notes about your day, including what lessons you learned and how you felt, can help you process your thoughts before you go to sleep.

Just like in the morning, I want to challenge you to try and not use your phone, or any other screen, in the hour before you go to bed for one week. Write down what you have done each day instead of using a screen during that hour. Thinking back to the beginning of this chapter, in both tasks, success will come down to your self-control.

Let the challenge begin!

The Power of Self-control

Hopefully by this point, you understand the power of using self-control and the positive effects it can have. If self-control is something you are already quite good at, don't keep your skills to yourself! You might have a younger sibling, a cousin or a friend who is not very good at practising self-control. They might not know how powerful and helpful it can be. But now you know what an amazing tool it is, you can speak up and be a positive influence.

As an adult, I am still practising self-control. It's something that never stops. It's a skill that we have to work on our whole lives. When I was younger, I used to be known as a hot head, but now I make the effort to keep my cool as often as I can. In frustrating or annoying situations, this can be a hard task, but that is where mastering self-control comes into play.

CHAPTER

WHAT ATTITUDE?

AN ATTITUDE IS A WAY OF THINKING OR FEELING ABOUT SOMETHING

In a family where there are brothers and sisters, there are certain roles that each kid is expected to fill. For example, the oldest child is usually the biggest, fastest and strongest one. The middle child can pretty much get away with anything – they're usually quiet and high expectations are not put on them. The youngest child is the spoiled one; everyone just thinks they're cute and adorable.

As the middle child, when I was little, I thought I wouldn't amount to much. Losing Stephen really changed my attitude. I started to put more effort into things. It gave me a driving force to choose a positive approach to life. Losing Stephen pushed me to see what I could achieve and succeed at. The fact that I was still here and he wasn't made me want to accomplish something in life. I wanted to make Stephen proud, because I knew he would want me to be great.

What Does Having an Attitude Mean?

An attitude is a way of thinking or feeling about something. You can have a bad attitude or a good attitude. With a bad attitude, you might be cheeky or uncooperative, like if your teacher asks you to stop talking in class and you keep answering back and rolling your eyes. With a good attitude, you might be helpful and friendly towards others.

"They have such an attitude!"

I bet you've heard something along those lines before. When **'attitude'** is used in this way, it means a **'bad attitude**. The person being talked about has usually misbehaved or been disrespectful.

At what age do you think you are able to make your own decisions? I have done loads of research on this and asked many young people the same question. I found out that you are able to make decisions much earlier than you might think. Are you ready for the answer? It's at four months old! Can you believe it? By four months old, a baby can make simple decisions, like choosing which grown-up they want to be cuddled by. If the wrong grown-up tries to pick them up, they let everyone know this was not their decision by starting to cry. By two years old, you've developed even more decision-making skills, making choices around your own behaviour, from what toy you want to use to who you want to play with. Let's fast forward to 13 years old. You have had 13 years of understanding and developing your decision-making skills. You've learned what is right and wrong, and understand what choices, attitudes and behaviours will lead to a negative or positive outcome.

Did you know that your attitude is purely your own choice? No matter what people say or do to you, you make the ultimate decision in how you will react. Sometimes, we act before taking a moment to think things over and make a balanced decision. It is usually better to make decisions based on logic and reason, rather than emotions. In future, try to pause for a minute, take a deep breath and think about your reaction before making any quick decisions.

I want you to understand that how much effort you put into something is often limited by your attitude. If you have a positive attitude, then you are more likely to put more effort into what you are doing. If you have a negative attitude, then you won't put in as much effort. How much effort are you willing to put in to succeed?

Can you think of something that you didn't quite put 100 per cent effort into, because you might have had a bad attitude at the time?

A Positive Attitude Creates Positive Results

Things that happen to you in life don't have to limit your goals. They are a part of your journey and something to learn from. Yes, some things are going to be difficult and challenging. Having the wrong attitude and listening to that little voice inside your head that says **"You can't do it"** or **"It's going to be too difficult"** is only going to hold you back from your never-ending possibilities. Remember, we all have this little voice and it's how we deal with it that counts. This is where your attitude becomes important.

Did you know that during your teenage years it's not only your body that changes, but your mind, too? Because of these changes, you will often sleep more than usual, and your emotions can sometimes feel scrambled. This is only temporary, and you shouldn't let those changes hold you back. Keeping a journal (which I will talk more about later in the book) can help you get those emotions out, almost like you are releasing them. Having a positive attitude can help, too, and will encourage you to keep everything in perspective.

Build That Positive Attitude

There are many ways that you can build a positive attitude. Here are a few ideas to get you started.

★ Give yourself compliments

Remember – you are your own superhero! Look in the mirror and tell yourself: **"I am my biggest competition"**, **"I am not lost, I'm still creating myself"** and **"I love myself unconditionally."** How does saying those things make you feel?

★ Keep a gratitude journal

Write down five things that you feel grateful for every day and see how your attitude changes. Our minds like to hold on to the negatives. We can have a great day and then one bad thing can happen that ruins everything. Writing down five positive things every day can help us keep things in perspective.

★ Mistakes can make you better

As you've seen in earlier chapters, with the right attitude, failures are just learning opportunities in disguise! We'll go into even more detail about this in the next chapter. You might receive a low score in a test but if you look over your mistakes and learn the correct answers, you'll get a better score next time.

★ Stop comparing yourself

Comparing yourself to other people only stops you from becoming the best version of yourself. When we compare ourselves, we focus on all the bits of our personalities or bodies that we don't feel measure up. We get jealous of other people, or start to feel bitter, and that creates a bad attitude. Everyone is unique and that is why you should only be in competition with yourself.

★ Stop staring at screens

Don't sit in front of a screen all day! It really affects your mood. It's been proven that people who spend less time on phones and tablets are way happier than people who are glued to their phones. They also get a lot more done.

Using your notepad, I want you to write down some things you are going to do every day to create a positive attitude and get yourself thinking 'yes' instead of 'no'. Here are a couple of ideas to get you started.

- Every day I'm going to give myself a compliment.
- Every day I'm going to try and make sure I have two hour away from screens.

After you've completed this activity, you'll be able to see the changes you want to make to build your positive attitude. You can use your list as a reminder.

Use Your Voice

So now you know the importance and power of your attitude – but don't keep the knowledge to yourself. If you have friends or family members who you feel do not have a positive attitude, or who don't put a lot of effort into things, you can encourage them and give them advice from this book. You never know, the friend or family member you encourage could be the next politician that creates positive change, the next lawyer to fight for someone's freedom or the next life-saving surgeon.

Like most people, I have been through personal challenges. I have dyslexia, and there were times when I wasn't able to complete tasks to my mum's extremely high standards. Even when I became an adult, I still had a feeling of falling short, but I made the decision to build a positive attitude. I focused on what I was good at and accepted what I was not so good at. We are not going to be good at everything and that is okay. I learned that it's not what other people think or say about me that matters, but what I think and say about myself.

If there are any words that I would like you to take away from this chapter, they would be:

Hard work beats talent, when talent doesn't work hard.

When you have a good attitude, that usually means you work hard and hard work, can only lead to success.

posi
atti

tive
tude

CHAPTER

IT'S NOT FAILURE, IT'S UNFINISHED BUSINESS

IN EVERY FAILURE THERE IS A LESSON TO BE LEARNED

My biggest failure after Stephen died was that I didn't take some time to process my feelings about what had happened. Instead of waiting a year to take my GCSEs, I decided to soldier on and do them straight away. I wasn't an A* student, but I was predicted to get good grades. But because I didn't give myself space, I ended up failing most of my exams. It was a massive blow, but after I sat down and thought about why it had happened, I realized that I needed to change my mindset and come up with a plan B.

I decided to go to a different college where things were a bit more relaxed, which I knew would work better for me. I completed a practical course equal to my GCSEs called a BTEC, which helped me to get into university. Hopefully, from this story, you can see that even though I failed some of the most important exams of my life, instead of giving up, I kept on fighting and found a different way to achieve my goals. Failure is not the end – 99 per cent of the time there is a solution!

FAIL: First Attempt in Learning

In every failure there is a lesson to be learned. When we fail, it's not the end; it's just our first attempt in learning! That's what I like to imagine the letters of 'fail' stand for.

Failure only becomes a problem when you keep making the same mistakes without changing your method or route. When we fail, it's important that instead of getting frustrated, angry or giving up, we sit back, look at why we failed and then find a solution.

Remember that little voice inside your head I was talking about? Well, sometimes it is supportive, and sometimes it puts doubt in your mind. Get into the habit of telling yourself positive things, instead of negative. After I'd failed my exams, I could have only listened to the negative voice telling me, "Stuart, don't waste your time, you'll only fail again." Instead, I listened to the positive one that told me to keep trying. I took my time thinking it over and came up with a solution to get my qualifications in a way that worked better for me.

Using your notepad, I want you to write down one thing that you feel you have failed at in the past. Did you give up? If you didn't try again, I want you to write down some ways that you could have tried to succeed a second time around.

Hopefully, this activity will show you that there is always a solution. Sometimes, we have to think long and hard about it. Sometimes the answer is right in front of us.

Turning Failure into a Positive

Here are some ways to think about failure and turn it into something positive.

★ Mistakes are not a problem, but not taking the opportunity to learn from them is a problem.

Spot your mistakes and learn from them quickly. Lots of successful people have experienced failure, but they build on those lessons they have learned. For example, Michael Jordan, one of the most famous basketball players in the United States, missed 9,000 shots and lost 300 games, but he kept on going to become one of the greatest players of all time. He once said, "If you quit once it becomes a habit. Never quit!"

★ Be careful about how you talk to yourself.

Talking negatively to yourself can be really damaging, especially after a failure. Take charge of the way you talk to yourself and don't let it make you feel rubbish. Let the failure sting for just a few seconds and then move on and speak positively to yourself.

★ It's better to do something imperfectly than to do nothing, perfectly.

The only true failure is doing nothing and not trying. When we do nothing, it means we are not moving or growing.

★ You don't have to let your mistakes define you.

Even if things don't go as planned, your future can still be better than you imagined. A lot of the time, we are afraid to talk about our failures and mistakes because we are scared that someone might use them to make us feel stupid or not good enough. If you are learning and thinking about how to win, then it doesn't matter what others think or say about you.

★ The enemy of success is the fear of failure.

It's not failing that's dangerous. It's being scared of failing that stops us from trying to do things. Like all fears, you beat it by facing it head on. Imagine you're learning to dive. After your tenth attempt, you are still doing belly flops. Perhaps you feel scared to try again – scared of the pain, of getting it wrong, of people laughing at you... But imagine you keep going and on the fifteenth attempt, bravo, you get it! Push through the fear, whatever it is you are trying to achieve.

★ Constant action creates constant results.

Strength does not come from what you can do, but from mastering the things you thought you couldn't do. When you fall down, learn to get up, dust yourself off, and move forward. What you do every day matters more than what you do every once in a while. Being able to keep on fighting and learning could and can be the keys to your success. Consistency and perseverance are character traits that come with time and patience, but you will get there in the end!

★ You can't always do it alone, and you don't have to.

Sometimes failing can keep us stuck in our ways. We need support to help us break our bad habits. The worst thing we can do is think we need to do things alone. If you're stuck, speak with a trusted adult. When you speak to someone who has had different experiences to you, they will be able to offer you a different point of view and help you to see what might be holding you back in your own situation.

Free Will

Free will is our ability to control our own actions and make our own choices. Though we have this freedom to make choices, we have to be sensible about the choices we make. After your mum or dad has just gone food shopping, the cupboard might be full to the brim with biscuits, chocolate and crisps. You have the free will to make the decision to eat all the snacks, and not save any for your other family members. But is this the right choice to make? Just because we can doesn't mean we should.

Here's another example. When picking your subjects at school, should you choose subjects because your friends will be in those classes? Or should you choose subjects because they are the ones that you enjoy, and the ones that will help you to get the career you want? It can be scary thinking you are not going to be with your friends in all your classes, but you'll most likely make new friends, and studying something you're passionate about is more important than having a chat anyway, which you can do at break! This is where being sensible comes into play. You need to make decisions that will help you get to where you want to go, so use your free will wisely.

Put Your Free Will to Use

WITH GREAT POWER COMES GREAT RESPONSIBILITY!

So, we've talked about the great power in our gift of free will. We've also talked about how failing can be a good thing. With this new understanding, I want you to speak up and help others. **Silence is not an option**. You may have a friend at school who is frustrated or upset because they've failed at something. Let them know that failure is not the end. They can learn from it and change their plans. It may even be your older siblings who feel like they have failed at something. Just because you are younger than them, doesn't mean you can't help them to see that good things can come through failure.

Failure is a part of life. Without it, there are a lot of lessons we would never learn. As humans, we are constantly trying to make everything perfect, but perfection can rarely be achieved. My idea of being perfect was soldiering on and doing my exams the day after losing my brother. I failed then, but I succeeded in the end. Through failure, I found I was better at hands-on work, not sitting at a table answering questions within a certain amount of time.

> When failure knocks at your door I want you to open it, sit down with it, then work out the solution to send it packing. Do not be beaten by it; learn from it. For lots of us, it's not that we aim too high and fail, but that we aim too low and succeed.

CHAPTER

DREAM BIG

WITHOUT DREAMING, YOU NEVER KNOW WHAT THE POSSIBILITIES COULD BE

I could imagine what Stephen would be like now, but that would be like jumping down a rabbit hole. Imagining would probably bring great sadness. Thinking about what he could have and would have been, along with all the moments and all the occasions we have missed out on sharing, is something I would find very hard.

Imagination, however, can also be a very good thing. Without dreaming, you never know what the possibilities could be.

The Importance of Your Imagination

I want you to think of your imagination as if it were a magician's hat, from which you can pick out ideas, goals and stories forever. Your imagination can take you anywhere; there is no end to it.

In your notepad, I want you to draw an aeroplane. Any kind of aeroplane is fine – there's no right or wrong. Once you have finished, I want you to label the picture with the answers to the questions below:

- What colour is the aeroplane?
- How many wheels does it have?
- What colour are the wheels?
- Where is it?

So, what kind of plane did you draw? We all know aeroplanes are usually white with black wheels, but someone with a very active imagination might draw a pink aeroplane with purple wheels. Perhaps your aeroplane was sitting waiting on a runway, or perhaps it was soaring over some mountains. The purpose of this activity is to highlight how endless your imagination can be. Maybe you limited your imagination and drew a plane you'd seen in real life. If that's the case, why not have another go and draw the most imaginative plane you can?

We need to learn not to limit our imaginations and instead keep our minds open to all kinds of possibilities. To have big dreams, we need to let our imaginations go wild.

Using your notepad, I want you to:

- Write down today's date
- Write down what you want to do as a job in the future
- Flick through magazines and leaflets to find pictures connected to what you want to do
- Cut out the pictures and stick them down underneath what you have written. You could also draw some of your own pictures, using your imagination.

Looking at what you have written down, where do you think that idea or goal comes from? It comes from your imagination. Without it, you wouldn't be able to imagine what you could be. That is why I want you to understand how important and powerful YOUR imagination is.

Life Without Phones

Do you know who Martin Cooper is? Martin invented the first handheld mobile phone, and he was the first person in the whole world to make a mobile phone call. Who did he call first? He called a competitor company, Bell Labs, to gloat that he had beaten them in the race to make the first mobile phone.

Can you believe that for a hundred years, people could only make calls through a telephone in their homes? Martin wanted to invent something that would make it easier for people to communicate while they were on the move. Without Martin's imagination, it's possible that, to this day, we would still be communicating using a wired telephone. Martin's story shows why imagination is so important. Even though others might try and force limits on you, if you can imagine and persevere, the possibilities of what you can achieve are endless.

Imagination is not just for 'creative people', but for everyone. During the Covid-19 pandemic, the entire world went into lockdown more than once. It was a difficult time for many, and lots of people lost their jobs. Imagination, however, played an important part in helping people to stay positive. Through their imagination, people came up with ideas for using their newfound free time effectively. Many set up new businesses from home, inspired by their passions and hobbies.

Make Those Big Dreams Real

Look again at what you have written down about what you want to do in the future. Do you know how to get there?

I want you to sit down with an adult that you feel comfortable talking to. This could be your big brother or sister, an aunt or uncle, or your mum or dad – someone that knows you well and will support your dreams. Together, write down three short-term, mid-term and long-term steps that can get you closer to the goal you have written down in your notepad. For example, if your goal is to become a professional football player, then the steps you could set yourself are:

Short-term steps:

1. Work on your footwork by practising drills in your garden or local park.
2. Watch player position-specific YouTube videos that are relatable to you, every day.
3. Practise stretching by trying activities like yoga.

Mid-term steps:

1. Alter your diet to eat more fruit and veg and less junk food.
2. Start other sports that help with strength and conditioning, such as swimming or gymnastics.
3. Try and sign up to a professional football academy.

Long-term steps:

1. Get an agent.
2. Apply for a scholarship contract for a professional football team.
3. Become a professional football player for Arsenal.

Use the above steps as a reminder of what you have got to do to get to where you want to go. The journey is going to be difficult. There are going to be times when you have to make decisions between short-term gains (like staying out late with your friends – you'll have fun, but you'll feel tired at practice the next day) and your long-term goals.

Fire Up Your Imagination!

To keep your imagination alive, you need to feed it. There are lots of ways to fire up your imagination so it can help you get to where you want to go. Don't forget, your imagination is a tool – so use it!

As you get older, your imagination can start to fade. This is why it's important to keep feeding it, so that it can help you to be the greatest version of yourself. Here are some ways to keep your imagination fired up:

★ Reading

Some people think reading means learning, and that it's just plain boring. But that's so not true. Books can give you a peek into other worlds, and those other worlds can help you to imagine what your future might hold.

★ Less screen time

As weird as this may sound, having easy access to screens like our phones, tablets, TVs and laptops doesn't give us the chance to be bored. When we are bored, that is when our creative flow kicks in. We do things to occupy ourselves and come up with new, out-of-the box ideas.

★ Daydreaming

For some of us, daydreaming comes naturally and it's actually hard to stop our minds wandering. For others, daydreaming is more of a deliberate action. It is a great way to open your mind to possibilities. When you have some spare time, maybe coming home on the bus or train, or when you are on holiday, try letting your mind wander. If you practise this often, it will soon become a habit. One day, your daydreaming might spark something for you, like an idea for a blog or a book, or a solution to a problem that might change people's lives.

★ Socializing

It's important to talk to and mix with other people from different backgrounds, so that you can learn from each other. The people you keep around you have a big influence on you. If you surround yourself with friends who have great imaginations, some of their creativity should hopefully rub off on you.

★ Listen

You don't always have to be the one with the big ideas. If you get the opportunity to be part of a project with lots of other people, pick their brains for ideas as well as sharing your own. If you listen to each other, all those imaginations working together could lead to something amazing.

★ Ask a question

If there are things you don't understand, ask! You should always ask questions like: Why? Where? How? What? Who? Finding out the full picture will help you to make sense of the world, and once you fully understand something, you can start dreaming up new ideas about it. When you start to ask questions, you might be surprised by what you learn.

★ Study

Don't limit your learning to school. Improving your knowledge and skills gives your imagination more freedom and sets you up for greatness. You could subscribe to podcasts or YouTube channels, or even join groups at your local library. When you learn a new skill or gain new knowledge it usually motivates you to try other new things.

★ Doodling

Help to relax your mind and get your creative juices flowing by having a little doodle when you are stressed, anxious or faced with a problem. Try to spark your imagination by practising 10 to 15 minutes of doodling each day. Just have fun and don't worry about creating a masterpiece – everyone's doodling style is unique.

My Own Experience

I never imagined that I would be a teacher, but I was – for 15 years! It was teaching young people that sparked the fire in my imagination to reach higher and inspire a bigger audience. It was those young minds that helped me find what I had a passion for and what I really wanted to do.

Now we've reached the end of this chapter, hopefully you understand and appreciate the importance of your imagination. If you were to silence and suppress your imagination, you could stop the world from benefitting from your brilliance. The inventions, ideas and plans you dream up could help to change the world for the better.

Your imagination is a tool – so use it!

→imagi

nation

CHAPTER

TAKE YOUR TIME

TIME
IS A TOOL
FOR
SUCCESS

Everyone's grief is personal to them. After Stephen's death, what I went through and how I dealt with it was different to my other family members. Time has been a great healer. It has allowed me to accept that there is nothing I could have or should have done. Time has allowed me to accept the idea that I won't see my big brother again, which is a massively hard reality to come to terms with.

I really want you to understand the concept of time. I want you to understand how important every minute is and what you can achieve when you plan with purpose. I also want you to think about what can happen if you don't put into practice what you have read in this book. It's so easy to end up 'wasting' time.

How Time Began

Have you ever wondered how people figured out the time before we had clocks? As early as 3500BCE, the ancient Greeks were building tall monuments called obelisks, which they used to tell the time. People watched the moving shadows, cast by the sun, to work out what time of day it was. Obelisks were not as accurate as modern clocks, but they helped people to divide the day up into two parts – before-noon and after-noon. Around 2,000 years later, the Egyptians invented the first proper sundial. Like obelisks, sundials used shadows to tell the time. But they divided the day into several chunks called hours.

This chapter would never end if we were to dive into all the wonderful ways people told the time in the past. Instead, let's get down to the business of how time can be used as a tool to help you succeed!

Good Time Management

Time is so important. Good time management will allow you to plan short-term and long-term goals effectively. These goals could be anything from making sure you wake up with plenty of time to get to your Saturday job, to planning your study schedule in order to pass your exams.

Using your notepad:

- Write down tomorrow's date and draw a timetable grid, with a row for every hour.

- Now plan out your whole day, hour by hour, from the time you are going to wake up to the time you are going to go to sleep. Make sure you include things like when you are going to have a shower, when you are going to eat breakfast and lunch, and what you are going to do every hour in between.

- If you have free time in your plan, think about what you could do with those spare hours or minutes. Sure, you could watch TV or mess around on a tablet, but is there anything more productive you could do that might help you achieve your life goals?

For example, if your aim is to work in the travel industry, you could use that spare time to start learning a new language. If you are interested in animals and wildlife, you might listen to a nature podcast to improve your knowledge. Hopefully this activity will help you to see how much you can get done in just one day! This doesn't mean you should squeeze in as many activities as you can every day, because we all need rest, but it will help you to see, and benefit from, the hours you might not have realized you had available.

Not everything you do today will benefit you tomorrow; sometimes the benefits take a little time to arrive, but they are worth the wait!

Poor Time Management

It's easy to put off doing something useful or productive and then look back and think, **"Oh, I could have done this"** or **"I should have done that."** Rather than making you feel bad, I want this chapter to inspire you to think about how you use your time. Have a chat with a trusted adult and ask them if there was ever an occasion when they wished they had used their time a bit more wisely. You will see that we all have these moments, but it is about limiting them and learning from them so that we can be the best versions of ourselves.

Poor time management can lead to bad decisions, regrets and upset. For example, you might decide to come home after school and binge-watch a new series instead of completing a bit of your coursework, which is due the next day. Before you know it, it's 9.30 p.m. You realize you haven't done the work and it's now too late to give it your best. In the long run, this small decision might lead to BIG regret, because it could end up affecting your grades and your prospects for the future.

Don't Let Time Slip Away

Time is something none of us can ever get back. If you waste an hour, it's gone, never to be seen again. Now that you have this knowledge, why not let your friends know? Empower them and influence change in them, too. It doesn't always have to be loud and proud, if that's not your way of doing things. For example, you and a friend may be the two kids that always turn up late at the beginning of the school day. You could suggest to your friend, "Do you want to meet at the bus stop at 8 a.m. instead of 8.20 a.m. tomorrow?" When you get to school slightly earlier, with time to pop your bag down and get settled, you should both feel less stressed. See how much more positive your day is just through this simple change. Hopefully, your friend will see the benefit of turning up on time as well.

My Own Experience

Growing up, I had a good friend who ended up spending some time in prison. One night, when he was out with his friends, he made a bad decision. He ended up getting involved in a fight where someone lost their life. My friend was convicted of manslaughter – the crime of killing a person by accident. He was sentenced to three and a half years in prison. He felt a lot of regret and guilt about what had happened, but there was no turning back time. He missed out on a lot of things, including seeing his young daughter grow up.

After serving his sentence, my friend turned his life around. He is now a role model to lots of people. However, think about all the amazing things he could have achieved if he hadn't lost those three and a half years.

THERE IS NO TURNING BACK TIME

CHAPTER

WHAT IS WEALTH?

IT'S SO IMPORTANT TO BE GRATEFUL FOR THE SIMPLE AND SMALL THINGS

I think losing Stephen so suddenly and tragically has shown me that I need to be grateful for the small things. There are things in life I am able to experience that Stephen never had the chance to, like getting married, having my son, finding my purpose and creating a career. With each of these new experiences, I remember Stephen.

It's so important to be grateful for the simple and small things. That's why I want you to understand the importance of gratitude and know that money is not everything.

Are You Rich?

I'm rich because of the family I have made for myself and the friends that I have. When I lost my brother, I realized that being rich or wealthy didn't just mean having lots of money. It meant having a home and being loved by friends and family, which no amount of money can buy. However, money is an important tool that, if you understand how to use it, can help you find your place and voice in the world.

Where Did Money Come From?

Before credit cards and online shopping, even before coins and banknotes, people used to trade things they felt were worth something. Let's say you made cloth. Imagine a farmer wanted some new clothes, and you wanted something to eat – the farmer could offer you a chicken in exchange for some fabric.

Over time, people travelled further to trade. Soon they needed something more portable to swap than chickens or cloth. They needed something that could be passed from person to person and hold its value. The first money – small, flat discs of silver or gold – was invented in around 600BCE in Lydia, which is now part of Turkey. The first coins were invented in China not long after. They had images stamped on them and different coins were worth different values. Today, there are around 180 different currencies around the world!

Working Smart, Saving Hard

As an adult, you'll need to earn money and set some of it aside for your future. Some jobs pay a lot of money and some pay less. The famous footballer Lionel Messi gets paid about £72,000 a day, while your local doctor makes less than that each year. However, you should follow your passions, rather than trying to get the highest pay cheque. There is no point becoming a banker just because it pays a lot, if you dislike maths and shudder at the idea of being stuck inside an office. On the other hand, if you love crunching numbers and travelling the world, banking might be for you. If you don't like your job, no amount of money will make you happy.

Saving money is really important, as you never know what is coming up around the corner in life. So, what's the best way to save? Imagine you've set up a lemonade stand. You're charging £1.80 for a cup of lemonade. Each cup has cost you £0.30 to make, so you are left with a profit of £1.50. Now, you can apply something called the **'principle of three'** to this.

Principle of Three

1. Spend a third
2. Save a third
3. Invest a third

So from your lemonade stand you have £0.50 to spend now, perhaps on a treat, £0.50 to put towards your future and £0.50 to invest. You can apply the same principles when you're a grown-up, and hopefully earning a bit more than £1.50! We all love to spend money. Some of us are good at saving towards something we really want, but we often forget to invest some of our money. This doesn't always mean investing in material things, but also investing in ourselves. Someone once said to me, "The most important project you will ever work on will be yourself." Those words sank in a couple of years ago. Since then, I have been trying to invest a bit more time, money and energy into myself. If I don't invest in myself and try to be the best I can be, then who am I expecting to do it for me? You can invest in yourself in lots of different ways, from buying books or equipment that improve your skills and learning, to signing up to a course. I recently invested in myself by taking a course in football coaching, which is an interest of mine.

The World of Work

There are lots of different ways you can earn money.

★ Self-Employed

You work by yourself and for yourself. Professionals who are often self-employed include plumbers, childminders, tutors, cab drivers, actors and hairdressers.

★ Employed

You are employed by a company or organization and paid a monthly wage, along with holiday pay and other benefits. Normally doctors, teachers, shop assistants and airline staff are employed.

★ Business Owner

Like someone who is self-employed, you work for yourself. If you are a business owner, you usually employ other people and manage a bigger organization, too. Business owners could run a company such as a salon, café, after-school club, plumbing company or nursery.

The most important project you will ever work on will be yourself.

Worth More Than Money

What do you think is the best kind of world? One where there are some rich people and some poor people, or one where everyone is equal? We live in a world where we are encouraged to try and make as much money as possible. When we do this, we sometimes forget the important things in life. Here are a few things that I think are more important than money:

★ Health

Without health there is no wealth. You can be as rich as anything, but if you are ill, tired or in pain, then you can't enjoy a penny of it. Health can't be bought – and we can help look after our health with the choices we make from eating healthily to regularly exercising.

★ Experiences

Many of life's greatest experiences are free. From appearing in a school play to going to grandma's birthday party, the amazing memories we make in life will make us way richer than money ever can.

★ Friendship

Friendship is so important. There is a common phrase, "Tell me who your friends are, and I'll tell you who you are." Your friends are a reflection of you, so make sure you surround yourself with people you admire and who support you. Building strong friendships can be much more rewarding than making lots of money.

★ Wisdom

Imagine being a millionaire without any wisdom or knowledge – I am pretty sure that your money would be wasted very quickly. Whereas you could be earning a normal salary and, by using your money wisely, become richer than a millionaire. Being curious about the world around you and learning new things is more fulfilling than being able to buy lots of meaningless items.

Grab your notebook and see if you can note down three more things that are more important in life than money.

Giving Back

If you're lucky enough in life to have more than enough money for yourself, it is important to put some of your wealth to good use. You could help communities that are less fortunate, donate to those who are in need or even set up your own charity.

There's something else we can all give that doesn't cost a thing – time! You don't even have to wait until you are an adult to do this. Each week, you could sacrifice an hour or two to give someone a hand. You could water a neighbour's garden, take out your family's bins or do a local litter pick. You could even offer to help clean a classroom or help a younger student study at lunchtime at school.

With your wealth, you have the option to help those who don't have the resources to have their voice heard. For example, let's talk about **Marcus Rashford**, the footballer who has been campaigning for vulnerable children and families since 2020. With his platform and influence, he was able to help children from vulnerable families receive free school meals during the half-term holidays. He also set up a children's book club and continues to campaign, fight and speak for those who don't always get listened to.

> # You have the option to help those who don't have the resources to have their voice heard

Being Rich Isn't Everything

In this chapter, hopefully you've learned that wealth is made up of much more than money. Having enough money to buy a house or a car and to be comfortable in life is great, but there are other more important things. Yes, everyone wants to be rich, but having good health, supportive friends and exciting life experiences is what really makes you a rich person who can make a positive impact on society and live a successful life. Share what you have, whether that is money or time, with your community. Start making changes right now that will set you up for the future.

CHAPTER

LIFELONG LEARNING

THERE IS
A LESSON
IN ALMOST
EVERYTHING

The biggest lesson I've learned since Stephen's murder is that tomorrow is not promised to anyone. I've learned to try and not waste a day, an hour or a minute. I've also learned that you should be nice to others and to take hold of new opportunities with both hands, whatever they might be.

What has been your biggest lesson in life? Did you learn it at school, at home, on holiday or when you were out with your friends?

There are two kinds of lessons. The ones you learn at school, and the lessons you learn on the journey of life. Both kinds of lessons are important in building the best version of you. As you get older, you begin to find that there is a lesson in almost everything. For example, your hand-eye coordination is developed by drawing and writing. You'll need good hand-eye coordination for all kinds of things in life, so good writing and drawing skills can lead on to you becoming a great artist, netball player, architect or surgeon. A lot of the time, we don't realize it's these little everyday skills that will eventually lead us to greatness.

Different Kinds of Learning

From our first day at school right through to our last day at university, most of our learning is based around a set curriculum. We make choices along the way, including what subjects we want to take for our GCSEs, and what we want to study at college or as an apprenticeship. As we get older, we tailor our learning so we can study the things we are most interested in. This helps us go into our chosen career or start our own business.

There are so many lessons you can learn outside of education. Lots of the time, you don't even notice the things you're learning. For example, if you decide to go travelling after completing school, it might feel like a fun holiday, but you'll also be gaining knowledge and wisdom. From building confidence when you buy a train ticket in another language to discovering how to cook a new cuisine, you are going to learn so many accidental lessons.

WE DON'T REALIZE IT'S THESE LITTLE EVERYDAY SKILLS THAT WILL EVENTUALLY LEAD US TO GREATNESS

Self-learning

Self-learning is anything you learn yourself, outside of the classroom. A great part of self-learning is the ability to satisfy your curiosity. Learning often happens naturally when we are curious about something, because we are excited to find answers ourselves. Self-learning becomes an adventure and your confidence grows each time you successfully learn something new. For example, if you want to become a cake maker, you might watch YouTube videos or download an app to develop your baking skills.

Where possible, it's great to learn things for yourself, rather than relying on other people. Let's say you go to Spain every summer. Luckily one of your parents speaks Spanish. Because they are always there to help you translate, you don't feel the need to learn the language. However, when you are older and decide to go to Spain with your friends instead, you no longer have your personal translator! This is where it would have been handy for you to use all those week-long holidays to learn Spanish, instead of depending on others to help you communicate.

Can you think of something you want to self-learn?

Life's Hidden Lessons

The hidden curriculum is a side effect of going to school. As well as the things you learn in class each day, you are also discovering new skills, values and perspectives without even knowing it. These lessons happen all the time through the conversations and interactions you have with your friends and teachers. Here are some lessons you might learn in school that are part of the hidden curriculum:

- Respecting other people's opinions
- Being reliable and on time
- Being competitive and wanting to achieve
- Understanding the value of hard work.

Even outside of school, we're still learning secret lessons all the time. Let's look at expectations in different cultures as an example. If you go to France, when greeting someone, you say "Bonjour!" and give the person a kiss on each cheek. In British culture, you just say "Hello!" and perhaps shake hands or give each other a pat on the back. It might be slightly odd if, next time you saw your friends, you tried to give them a kiss on the cheek – but it wouldn't be odd if you lived in France. You learn these small social lessons simply from spending time with other people.

Different cultures have different expectations about what

is considered respectful and disrespectful. Did you know that in Ghanaian culture, if you offer or receive items with your left hand it's considered a disrespect because your left hand is thought of as your 'toilet hand'? In British culture, however, it's not disrespectful to receive or give items using your left hand. When you meet people from other cultures, try to be aware that they might see things differently to you. If you're unsure whether a gesture or term is offensive, you can always ask.

Most of us try hard to fit in with others. It takes a level of awareness to notice all these little social expectations, but once you know them, you can really use them to your advantage. Being socially aware can help you to interact with all different kinds of people in life. Like we have discussed in previous chapters, it's so important to interact and connect with all sorts of people, because we can all learn from each other.

Using your notepad, I want you to write down three things:

1. An expectation in your culture.

2. A positive or negative experience you've had because of your race.

3. An expectation you think others have of you, because of your age.

My examples are:

1. In my culture, I'm expected to be respectful. I have to go and say hello to my elders first, or if I am told to do something, I am expected to do it. This is expected of me as a younger person in the family, and as part of my Caribbean culture.

2. My love for cooking came from making food with my great-aunt, who was from Jamaica. We created some great memories while cooking and without my Jamaican heritage I wouldn't have had those same experiences.

3. At my age, people expect that I will have my whole life sorted. They think that I should be married, have a house, have a good career and have kids.

I want you to complete this activity so that you can see how great it is to be different and unique because of where you come from. It's also good to acknowledge the expectations, good or bad, that people have of us for different reasons.

Soft and Hard Skills

There are different kinds of skills that we gain in life. Hard skills refer to the things we can do, like speak a language or use a computer programme, whereas soft skills are more about our personality traits. Hard skills might get you a job, but soft skills will help you to thrive in the job.

Here are some examples of hard skills:

- Being able to use a computer

- Knowing how to code

- Speaking a foreign language

- Having a university degree.

Did you notice that a lot of these skills are things you can be taught? Usually, you'll learn hard skills in the classroom, through books and other training materials, or when you get a job.

Here are some examples of soft skills:

- Communication skills – the way we listen and talk to other people

- Teamwork – how we work in a group

- A positive attitude – the way we act, and the level of effort we bring to a task

- Creativity – how imaginative and interesting our ideas are

- Emotional intelligence – the ability to tell how other people are feeling.

These skills allow us to work well with others, perform well in tasks and achieve goals. Soft skills are usually learned from family, friends and teachers without us even realizing we are learning them.

It's Not Always What You Know, But Who You Know

It might seem strange that I, a former teacher, am telling you this, but there is some truth in the statement above. There are so many benefits to knowing people from all different walks of life. For example, when you come to do work experience, you might want to work in that sports industry. If you already know somebody working in this area, they could help you get your foot in the door. This is all the more reason to be polite to your friend's mum, kind to the kids in the year below you at school and respectful to everyone new you meet – you never know when you might need their help in life!

The Power of Lifelong Learning

Learning is not only based in the classroom. You can learn at home or on the street, with your friends and by yourself. There are lessons to be learned everywhere you turn; and it's how you use those lessons that is important. Encourage your friends to self-learn and teach them why it is important to improve their skills and increase their knowledge. Encourage them to take up opportunities, even if they are outside of their comfort zone. Speak up to encourage and empower others with the knowledge you take from this chapter.

WE CAN ALL LEARN FROM EACH OTHER

CHAPTER

BEFORE
I GO

NEVER DOUBT HOW AMAZING YOU ARE, AND WHAT YOU CAN BRING TO THIS WORLD

So we have come to the end of our journey together and I hope you are feeling excited about your future and ready to go! Each chapter has given you tools to build a successful future for yourself, learn something new and charge forward in this ride called life.

The Power of Your Notepad

In each chapter, I have asked you to do an activity in a notepad. To take this further, you could start a journal that you try to write in each day. Journalling is not only useful for planning out goals, but it is also helpful to write down how you feel. You could even make a mood board or poster, covered in inspirational quotes and images, and stick it up in your bedroom. This could help remind you of the goals you set while reading this book. This is something that, along with this book, you can look at every day; something that will keep you focused on where you are going and what you want to become.

Look back at the exercises you did for each chapter every now and then and see if anything has changed. For example, you might remember that in Chapter 6 I asked you to write down the date and what career or job you want to have when you are older. Over time, your ambitions might change. Right now, you might want to be an architect, but in a year or two, perhaps you'll want to be an interior designer instead. As life goes on, you'll meet new people and learn new things, so it's no wonder some of your goals will change. That is what makes life so exciting!

Use this book every now and then to remind yourself of the powerful tools you've learned. If you find yourself falling back into the habit of wasting time, grab **Silence is Not an Option** and re-read Chapter 7 for motivation and guidance. If you feel your imagination is fading, re-read the Chapter 6 and reawaken your creativity. Look back at the notes you made to reaffirm your passions and your goals.

Your New Tools for Life

By reading this book and self-reflecting, I hope you see that you are amazing. You have incredible potential and I hope that some of the tools in this book will help you achieve that potential. Here's a reminder of just a few of the tools you've been given:

Self-reflection

In each chapter I have asked you to take part in some activities that make you self-reflect, which means thinking about your own feelings and behaviour. Self-reflection helps us to celebrate our strengths and work on our weaknesses.

Self-love

Being kind to yourself is so important! As we talked about in Chapter 1, you are your own superhero. Try to remind yourself of that as often as you can and celebrate your amazing uniqueness.

Self-discipline

Being disciplined will drive you to work hard. Knowing when to turn off the screens and get some work done is a powerful skill.

Silence is Not an Option

Now that we have come to the end of the book, I want you to take the opportunity to pass on your newfound wisdom to your friends and family members. There is an old saying **"love for your brother what you love for yourself"**, so if you want to be successful, you should want this for your siblings, your close friends and anyone else you meet in life. While reading, you might feel there are tips in the book that you can recommend to others. Don't be silent, let others know and help them to become the best version of themselves. We can all be great together!

Imagine the possibilities that you have with these new tools for life. You have the power to create change. Never doubt how amazing you are, and what you can bring to this world. If Martin Cooper doubted how amazing he was, who knows, maybe we wouldn't have mobile phones today. If Nelson Mandela didn't believe he could bring change to South Africa, maybe apartheid would still exist.

BELIEVE IN YOURSELF ALWAYS AND GIVE MORE TO THE WORLD THAN YOU TAKE FROM IT

ABOUT THE

Stuart Lawrence is a motivational speaker and youth engagement specialist. His brother, Stephen Lawrence, was murdered in a racially motivated attack in 1993. The Lawrence family's tireless campaign for justice has led to cultural shifts and changes in attitudes towards racism within British society.

Stuart worked as a teacher for fifteen years. He now works within the education system to equip young people with the mindset to believe and achieve what they want in life, no matter the challenges they might face.

With the Stephen Lawrence Foundation, Stuart helps to promote Stephen Lawrence Day, marked each year on 22 April – the day in 1993 that Stephen died. Stephen Lawrence Day is a celebration of his life and legacy; a moment to reflect, to keep the focus on racial inequality and celebrate efforts to remove it.

AUTHOR

INSPIRATION

Here's a selection of books and people who have inspired me on my journey through life.

A good book to read:

Long Walk to Freedom by Nelson Mandela – there is an abridged edition available for young readers.

See if any of these authors are on your bookshelves at school:

Julia Donaldson
Dr Seuss
Roald Dahl
Malorie Blackman

For inspiration, check out:

Omari McQueen
Instagram: @omarimcqueen
A young entrepreneur who started his own vegan food business and has his own TV show and cookbook publishing.

Greta Thunberg
Instagram: @gretathunberg
A young campaigner fighting to save our planet in the fight against global warming.

Timothy Armoo
Instagram: @timarmoo
A young entrepreneur who is the Chief Executive Officer of one of the world's leading marketing agencies.

Stormzy
www.stormzy.com
A rapper who rapidly shot to fame and has used his platform to give back to his community through initiatives such as university scholarship funds.

Farzana Khan
Twitter: @khankfarza
A writer and the co-founder and executive director of Healing Justice London, an organization aiming to heal communities and break down barriers.

David Olusoga
Twitter: @DavidOlusoga
A British historian, writer, broadcaster, presenter and filmmaker.

Barack Obama
Instagram: @barackobama
The first black President of the United States of America, who fought to break down barriers by winning the seat for presidency.

Michelle Obama
Instagram: @michelleobama
Although her husband was the 44th President of the United States, Michelle Obama has been successful in her own right as a lawyer and writer.

It would be great to hear what you think of this book. If you have any questions you can contact me at:

@Hon_stuartlawrence on Instagram and Tiktok
@sal2nd on Twitter
@hon_stuartlaw on Snapchat

Stay Safe Online

Please remember the golden rules of online life:

- Think about waiting until you're 13 to use social media.
- Keep your location and personal information private.
- Be smart – don't agree to meet face-to-face with an online friend, or send them photos of yourself, until you've spoken to an adult your trust.
- Report anything abusive or that makes you feel uncomfortable to a trusted adult.
- Remember your digital footprint – everything you post online is permanent.

ACKNOWLEDGEMENTS

I dedicate the words in this book to the following.

My son, Theo.

I must mention my beautiful and patient wife Angie. You know me better than I know myself and I appreciate all that you are to me and to Theo, for we are both lucky to have you on our team, fighting our corner.

My mum, Georgina Mia and Ethan.

To my family, who have always been with me through the good and the bad – they believed in me more than I sometimes believed in myself.

Ian Downes, a special person who I owe a great debt of gratitude and appreciation to. He sees in me what I wish the whole world could.

NW, aka The Wordsmith massive, thank you for being there and making sure that I was not going down the yellow brick road of madness and staying on track.

Sean Kitchlu-Connolly, who from what I know has a super bright future ahead of him. Thank you for your insight.

Also, thanks has to go to:

Elvin Oduro

Steve Randell

Charlotte Ansell

Man Dem Group

All the people that I asked random questions of.

All the kids that took part in the Scholastic questionnaire.

The Scholastic team.

And to my brother Stephen. I had you with me on Earth for sixteen years, but always will be in my heart and mind forever.

You are my SUPERHERO.

Stuart Lawrence

INDEX